THE JOURNEY OF ONE DETERMINED EDUCATOR

Dr. Michael Copeland

Award-Winning Author

CONTENTS

Dedication 4

Preface 6

Chapter 1: The Beginning 10

Chapter 2: Going to College 15

Chapter 3: The Camp Year 1 21

Chapter 4: Year 2 and a Vision Unfolds 29

Chapter 5: The Turning Point 38

Chapter 6: Impact and Challenges 46

Chapter 7: A Legacy in the Making 55

Chapter 8: Navigating the Professional Landscape 60

Chapter 9: Innovations in Education 65

Chapter 10: Beyond Classroom Walls 71

Chapter 11: Advocating for Systemic Change 78

Chapter 12: The Impact Unfolds 84

Chapter 13: The Next Generation of Educators 90

Chapter 14: Reflections and Legacy 96

Conclusion: The Ever-Evolving Journey 103

DEDICATION

This book is dedicated to the pillars of my life—my wife, Dr. Joi Stallworth Copeland, and my parents, Terence Copeland and Margot James Copeland. Your unwavering support, love, and encouragement have been the driving forces behind my journey. Joi, your partnership is my greatest strength, and your love fuels my passion for making a difference. Mom and Dad, your belief in education and the values you instilled in me have been my guiding light. This book stands as a tribute to the endless inspiration you provide. Thank you for being my foundation and constant source of strength.

PREFACE

In the tapestry of life, threads of adversity, resilience, and redemption weave a narrative that transcends the ordinary. As I embark on the journey of recounting the experiences and revelations that shaped my path, I invite you into the world of "The Journey of One Determined Educator"

The protagonist of this tale, James Turner, emerges from the shadows of a tumultuous adolescence to navigate the intricate realms of education. Born in the heart of Cleveland, Ohio, James grapples with challenges that threaten to eclipse his potential. As the youngest of three children, he battles academic mediocrity, personal demons, and a search for purpose that takes him to the brink of despair.

Surrounded by a supporting cast that includes the unwavering love of his parents, the success of his siblings, and the turbulence of a misguided youth, James embarks on a transformative odyssey. His journey, however, is not a solitary one. Alongside him are mentors like the indomitable Master Sergeant, whose wisdom guides James through the chaos of a summer camp that becomes a crucible of change.

In the tapestry, a myriad of characters enriches the narrative — family members, mentors, colleagues, and the young souls whose lives intersect with James in profound ways. Each character contributes a unique hue to the canvas, forming a vibrant palette that paints the picture of an educator's evolution.

The supporting characters include James's family: his parents, Mr. and Mrs. Turner, whose belief in education becomes a cornerstone; siblings whose success casts shadows and illuminates' paths; and the extended family that accompanies James on the exhilarating journey to Central State University, where the legacy of education takes root.

The Master Sergeant, a beacon of discipline and mentorship, becomes a pivotal figure in James's life during the chaotic first week of the summer camp. His guidance transcends the camp, leaving an indelible mark on James's approach to education.

As the journey unfolds, new characters grace the stage — fellow educators, students, and advocates for change. Each plays a role in the ever-evolving narrative of an educator's pursuit of resilience and impact. The protagonists and antagonists in this story are not merely individuals but embodiments of ideologies, systemic challenges, and societal norms that shape the landscape of education.

As you turn the pages of "The Journey of One Determined Educator," envisage the characters not as figments of imagination but as echoes of real people navigating the complexities of an educational odyssey. Join James Turner and his ensemble as they confront adversity, celebrate triumphs, and strive to redefine the narrative of education.

May this preface serve as an invitation into a world where the characters are not confined to pages but resonate in the collective journey of educators, students, and advocates who dare to dream of a brighter, more equitable future through the transformative power of education. The odyssey awaits, and the characters beckon you to witness the unfolding chronicle of resilience and education.

Chapter 1:

THE BEGINNING

I grew up in Cleveland, OH. I was the youngest of three children. We came from a good household and parents who were actively involved in our lives and had a strong belief in education. My siblings were always very successful in school and everything they did. I, however, was not. It seemed like everything was a struggle for me school, sports, friendships, ext. I always had mediocre grades throughout high school. I graduated by the skin of my teeth with a 2-point-nothing GPA. I slacked off, got high, and got in trouble with the wrong crowd.

The summer I graduated high school, I was so depressed because I did not get accepted into any out-of-state schools due to my grades, my ex-girlfriend got pregnant and decided to abort the baby, and hanging with the wrong crowd got me arrested for illegal activity multiple times. That summer I had no idea what I wanted to do with my life, so I decided I had no purpose and to end my life. One day, I came home from a long day, and we lived in an apartment building, so I took myself to the fifth-story balcony and threw myself off the building. That was my first real suicide attempt. When I hit the ground, it made a loud thud which woke up several neighbors. The neighbors rushed out to see what had happened in panic. Next thing you know I see the ambulance and police running to the backyard of the apartment where I landed.

My family was notified, and I was immediately taken to the hospital. When I arrived at the hospital My parents and sister were there. The look of devastation on my mother's face, my sister's face, and My father's face is something that will never forget as long as I live. I had hurt them, I had scared them, and I made everyone concerned beyond belief. Before my suicide attempt, I didn't even consider the impact that it would have on my family. After I was checked out at the hospital, they immediately sent me to a psychiatric ward for suicidal patients so I could receive help. I spent seven days in the psychiatric ward with individuals just like me depressed. I completed my therapy lessons and all the requirements to get released. I was still required to seek outside therapy upon my exit from the ward and I was placed on antidepressant pills. When I returned home, I knew something had to change! I had to create a new lifestyle for myself. This is when I chose to give my life back to Christ and got saved. I started attending church a lot more, bible study, and praying more and it truly made a difference for my future. I should have been dead, but God spared my life.

This was when I realized I had a purpose for my future and God had a plan. I went to community college in Cleveland for a year. Even though I did not get into any out-of-state schools, I did get into all in-state schools. The next year, I chose to attend an HBCU in my home state of Ohio called Central State University.

Chapter 2:

GOING TO COLLEGE

Central
State
University
1 8 8 7 ®

As I am preparing to leave for college feeling anxious, my family provided me with a great send-off! We had a wonderful graduation party the day before I hit the road and was showered with gifts, inspiration, and all the tools I needed to have a fresh start on my own. It has been a family tradition that whenever a child goes off to college the family goes with them on the first day to help them set up the room in the college dorm.

My entire family including my 91-year-old grandfather drove with me down to Central State University. It was such an exciting time! I had my mom, dad, brother, sister, grandmother, aunt, cousin, and grandfather. This took place one year before he passed away. My grandfather only had an 8th-grade education then went on to the army and served in World War 2. It was great for him to see his youngest grandson be a second-generation college student.

My dad was the first generation graduating from Harvard. No pressure, right? Lol. I knew I had a high standard to meet but after all I had been through after high school, I was ready to take on this challenge and start a new life.

I met my college roommate two months before the move-in date at orientation. He was a younger

16-year-old who came out of an accelerated program. I was 18 years old, so it felt like having a little brother. We became great friends and supported each other through freshmen year. I loved college and had so much fun during my freshmen year! I knew that if I wanted to stay here, it would require me to get focused on my grades for real. I worked harder than I ever had worked in my life starting my first semester at Central. I went to every class and sat in the front row of those classes. I never missed an assignment or paper. I was proud of myself for the first time in my life. I worked hard all semester and when it ended, I saw something I never had seen before. It was a 3.8 GPA on my report card.

I also had been awarded the Top Scholar award through my major in the Education department. I couldn't believe it nor could my parents. I said to myself, so this is the result of what hard work looks like. At the end of the first semester, I also started dating my college sweetheart. This relationship would last throughout college, but it turned into hell on wheels and became another challenge I would have to overcome. Even though I had started dating, I didn't let that distract me. After receiving that first semester GPA, I was determined to stay the course! I worked just as hard in the second semester and received the same GPA. I had now made the Dean's list two semesters in a row and completed my freshmen year.

I was able to bring home my Top Scholar award to show my grandfather. By this time, he was completely bedridden and barely spoke, but he could see and hear. It felt good to give him his flowers while he was here. I knew I wanted to stay involved with the school over the summer, so I looked into getting a summer job through the education department. I found a job as a camp counselor through the Urban Education Initiative. Little did I know that would be a life-changing journey for me throughout college.

Chapter 3:

THE CAMP YEAR 1

The Talented Tenth

W E B DuBois

"Talented Tenth"

- "The Negro race, like all races, is going to be saved by its exceptional men. The problem of education, then, among Negroes must first of all deal with the Talented Tenth; it is the problem of developing the Best of this race that they may guide the Mass away from the contamination and death of the Worst."

It is now summer of 2008 and I was on my way back to college after being home for a short break in May. I returned to school this summer for my job as a camp counselor. When I got to the school, I entered the gym where the kids were placed. The kids were from all over the state of Ohio. They were from the urban areas of Cleveland, Cincinnati, Columbus, and Dayton.

When I walked in, the first counselor that saw me said "Man, I hope you got some big balls for this job!". From that point, I had no idea what I had signed up for. We were in for a rude awakening. The youth were told to head to the auditorium and when they got in there, they were all over the place clowning each other, cussing, fighting, running around, making a mess of the room. I along with a couple of other new counselors raised our voice at them several times but that didn't make a difference.

With the environments that they came from, what they were used to anyway, being yelled at by authority figures. As new counselors and young college students ourselves, we had no idea what to do. The entire camp was chaotic and unorganized that whole first week. In my head thought "This is going to be a long three weeks just for a couple hundred dollars! ". As I was struggling that first week, I met the Master Sergeant who happened to be hired as a consultant for the summer camp.

Little did I know that he would become one of my biggest mentors. He was a former marine, so he knew how to get everything in line. He encouraged me to get to know the kids in my group by having one-on-one conversations. When I did that, each kid opened up to me. This blew my mind! Something so simple that I failed to do in the first place worked! I was also open with them about my struggles as a kid. These kids were not going to listen to me or anyone if they did not have a relationship with us. Building relationships with your students is key! Once the relationship was there and they saw that I was being real with them, they would do anything you asked of them including going to the summer classes and doing the assignments. That first week was a struggle but I was thankful for the progress I made by actually getting to know my students! After that, the rest was history.

We taught those young men etiquette, academics, and the history of famous African Americans. We even had each group named after a famous African American and the students had to research information on the famous person in history and recite accurate information when asked at any given time through the camp days by any instructor. We also created a rites of passage class which taught the young men about slavery, the middle passage, all the way to the underground railroad. The Young men heard what slaves would hear and what they went through which brought a lot of the young men to tears. It was such a humbling experience for them. This would later become the start of each camp in the coming years. We became so well organized and structured from that first week of chaos that you could see the progress in each of the young men at the end.

Since we had taught the young men classes on etiquette, we had a formal gala for them at the end of each camp week. We had them dress up and eat in a nice formal setting in the college ballroom. That was a first-time experience for most if not all young men. I had one young man in my group, and he was my group leader. He had never received a haircut, so I took him to get his first haircut on campus before the gala. That made his day! These young men had such life-changing experiences at our camp that we knew we had to keep this going for future summers.

Chapter 4:

YEAR 2 AND A VISION UNFOLDS

children's
defense fund
FREEDOM SCHOOLS®

Habakkuk 2:2
...Write the vision...
DREAM
VISION

As I entered my sophomore year at Central State University, my experiences from the camp and freedom schools continued to shape my perspective on education. The passion for making a positive impact on the lives of inner-city youth burned within me. I declared my major in Education with a focus on Urban Education, determined to bring change to the communities that needed it most.

During the school year, I became actively involved in various education-related initiatives on campus. I joined student organizations, participated in volunteer programs, and collaborated with professors who shared my vision. The fire that was lit during that transformative summer burned brighter with each passing day.

Vision is the unfolding of God's master plan, whereas direction is the steps you take to accomplish it.
David O. Oyedepo

As I delved deeper into my studies, I discovered the power of mentorship. Remembering the impact the Master Sergeant had on me during the chaotic first week of camp, I sought out opportunities to mentor others. I became a mentor for incoming freshmen, sharing my story of resilience and redemption. Through these interactions, I realized the potential to inspire change in young minds by simply being there for them.

I found myself immersed in a period of reflection and transformation. The experiences of the previous year, particularly my time as a camp counselor, had left an indelible mark on my psyche, igniting a fervent passion for education and social change. With each passing day, my resolve strengthened, propelling me towards a future dedicated to uplifting inner-city youth and challenging systemic inequities.

The summer following the camp was a pivotal moment in my journey. I seized the opportunity to immerse myself further in the realm of education by taking on a role as a servant leader intern/teacher for freedom schools in Cleveland. The program, rooted in the principles of social justice and community empowerment, provided a platform to engage with more inner-city youth and amplify their voices.

Despite my fervent dedication to the cause, the path was not without its obstacles. I encountered resistance from a superior who seemed intent on thwarting my efforts and undermining my commitment. His power trip threatened to derail my aspirations and dampen my spirit. However, in the face of adversity, I refused to waver. I fought tooth and nail to overcome the challenges, recognizing that obstacles are merely opportunities in disguise.

The experience at the freedom schools served as a crucible, refining my vision and fortifying my resolve. I witnessed firsthand the transformative power of education when coupled with genuine passion and unwavering dedication. The connections forged with students transcended the confines of the classroom, fostering a sense of trust, empowerment, and mutual respect.

Armed with renewed purpose and a deeper understanding of the complexities inherent in urban education, I entered my sophomore year at Central State University with unwavering determination. My major in Education with a focus on Urban Education became a beacon guiding my path forward. I was determined to challenge the status quo, dismantle systemic barriers, and pave the way for a brighter future for underserved communities.

Throughout the school year, I immersed myself in various education-related initiatives on campus, eager to translate my passion into tangible action. I joined student organizations, participated in volunteer programs, and sought out opportunities to collaborate with professors who shared my vision. The fire that was kindled within me during that transformative summer burned brighter with each passing day, propelling me towards my ultimate goal of effecting meaningful change.

Central to my journey was the realization of the power of mentorship. Reflecting on the profound impact the Master Sergeant had on me during the tumultuous first week of camp, I sought out opportunities to pay it forward. Becoming a mentor for incoming freshmen, I shared my story of resilience and redemption, offering a guiding hand to those navigating the tumultuous waters of higher education. Through these interactions, I discovered the transformative potential inherent in simple acts of empathy, compassion, and understanding.

As I reflect on the journey that led me to this point, I am filled with a sense of gratitude and purpose. The experiences of the past year have shaped my perspective, fortified my resolve, and illuminated the path forward. With unwavering determination and a steadfast commitment to justice and equity, I stand poised to embark on the next chapter of my journey—a journey fueled by passion, guided by purpose, and dedicated to empowering the voices of those who have been silenced for too long.

Chapter 5:

THE TURNING POINT

One day, while attending a seminar on educational equity, I was introduced to a program that aimed to address the educational disparities in underprivileged communities. The program focused on training and placing student educators in schools where resources were scarce, but the potential was abundant. This was also a part of the education major requirements. This was also a turning point for me. I saw it as an opportunity to directly contribute to the change I wanted to see.

ELEMENTARY SCHOOL

I applied for the program and, to my delight, was accepted. The summer before my junior year, I found myself in a new city which was Dayton, OH, ready to embark on a journey that would test my abilities and commitment. I was placed in a school where students faced numerous challenges, but I was determined to make a difference.

In the midst of this transformative journey chronicled in this narrative, the stories of young black males overcoming struggles and fights in school are interwoven, highlighting the profound impact of dedicated educators and supportive communities.

Among the students I encountered during my time as a student teacher, there were numerous instances where challenges seemed insurmountable. However, it was through perseverance, empathy, and innovative approaches to education that these young men found their path to success.

One such story is that of Malik, a high school sophomore struggling with anger management issues and academic apathy. Malik's journey began with frequent clashes with authority figures, fights with peers, and a general sense of hopelessness about his future. Despite his outward bravado, Malik harbored deep-seated insecurities and a fear of failure.

As his student teacher, I recognized the potential within Malik, buried beneath layers of trauma and societal expectations. Through one-on-one mentoring sessions, I encouraged Malik to express his emotions constructively and provided him with the tools to navigate conflict resolution. Together, we explored his interests and strengths, channeling his energy into creative outlets such as poetry and spoken word.

Over time, Malik's demeanor began to shift. He developed a sense of self-awareness and resilience, learning to advocate for himself and seek support when needed. Academic interventions tailored to his learning style and interests allowed Malik to excel in areas where he once struggled. With each small victory, his confidence grew, and the cycle of negativity that once defined his experience in school began to dissipate.

The turning point came when Malik participated in a school-wide poetry slam competition. His powerful words resonated with his peers, offering a glimpse into his inner struggles and the resilience that defined his journey. As he stood on stage, baring his soul to the audience, Malik realized the transformative power of storytelling and the catharsis of self-expression.

From that moment on, Malik became a beacon of hope for his peers, sharing his story and inspiring others to overcome their own challenges. He formed a poetry club, providing a safe space for students to explore their emotions and creative potential. Through his leadership and unwavering determination, Malik not only transformed his own life but also ignited a movement within his school community.

Malik's story is just one of many examples of young black males overcoming adversity in the face of systemic challenges. Through targeted interventions, mentorship, and a commitment to equity and inclusion, educators can empower students to rewrite their narratives and realize their full potential.

As I reflect on the impact of my journey as an educator, I am reminded of the resilience and strength exhibited by students like Malik. Their stories serve as a testament to the transformative power of education and the unwavering belief in the potential of every individual, regardless of their background or circumstances.

In the ever-evolving landscape of education, it is imperative that we continue to champion the voices of those who have been marginalized and underserved. By fostering a culture of inclusivity, empathy, and support, we can create a more equitable and just society for future generations.

Chapter 6:

IMPACT AND CHALLENGES

During my student teaching, my days were filled with lesson planning, engaging with students, and addressing the unique needs of each individual. The bond I formed with my students was powerful, and I could see the impact of my efforts on their academic and personal growth.

However, the journey was not without its challenges. Limited resources, societal issues, and bureaucratic hurdles were constant obstacles. Yet, I persevered, drawing strength from the resilience of my students and the passion that fueled my mission.

As the school year progressed, I initiated community outreach programs, collaborated with local organizations, and advocated for educational reforms. Slowly but surely, change was happening, not just within the walls of the classroom but in the broader community.

The summer had been a period of profound reflection and transformation, fueled by the experiences that had shaped my journey as an aspiring educator. With a renewed sense of purpose and a fervent commitment to making a difference, I eagerly anticipated the challenges and opportunities that lay ahead.

The echoes of my time as a camp counselor still

resonated within me, serving as a constant reminder of the transformative power of education. Armed with this newfound perspective, I seized the opportunity to immerse myself further in the realm of educational outreach by taking on a role again as a servant leader intern/teacher for freedom schools in Cleveland. This would be my third year doing Freedom Schools. Little did I know that this experience would further deepen my understanding of the challenges facing inner-city youth and ignite a passion for advocacy and social justice.

As I stepped into the classroom, I was confronted with the stark realities of poverty and inequality that many of my students faced on a daily basis. For them, education was not merely a pathway to success but a lifeline in the face of adversity. I encountered students who grappled with homelessness, hunger, and the crushing weight of economic insecurity, yet remained steadfast in their pursuit of knowledge and opportunity.

One student, Jamal, stands out in my memory. He arrived at school each day with a smile on his face, despite the fact that he often slept in shelters and relied on free meals provided by the school for sustenance. Despite the challenges he faced, Jamal was determined to succeed, fueled by a relentless drive to break free from the cycle of poverty that had ensnared his family for generations. His resilience and determination served as a constant source of inspiration, reminding me of the transformative power of education to uplift and empower even in the face of seemingly insurmountable odds.

As my days became filled with lesson planning, engaging with students, and addressing the unique needs of each individual, I found myself drawn deeper into the intricacies of their lives. The bond I formed with my students was powerful, transcending the traditional roles of teacher and student to become a source of mutual support and encouragement. Together, we navigated the complexities of the educational landscape, confronting limited resources, societal issues, and bureaucratic hurdles with unwavering determination and resolve.

Despite the challenges we faced, I refused to succumb to despair. Instead, I initiated community outreach programs, collaborated with local organizations, and advocated for educational reforms that would address the systemic inequities that perpetuated poverty and inequality. Slowly but surely, change began to take root, not just within the walls of the classroom but in the broader community as well.

Through our collective efforts, we forged a path forward, guided by a shared commitment to justice, equity, and opportunity for all. Together, we confronted the obstacles that threatened to derail our progress and emerged stronger and more resilient than ever before. As the school year progressed, I witnessed the transformative impact of our efforts on the academic and personal growth of my students, their voices echoing the promise of a brighter future forged through education and empowerment.

Though the journey was fraught with challenges and obstacles, I remained steadfast in my belief that education had the power to transcend barriers and unlock the boundless potential that lay within each and every one of us. As I reflect on the year that had passed, I am filled with a sense of gratitude for the opportunity to make a difference in the lives of my students and a renewed sense of purpose as I prepare to embark on the next chapter of my journey—a journey fueled by passion, guided by purpose, and dedicated to empowering the voices of those who have been silenced for too long.

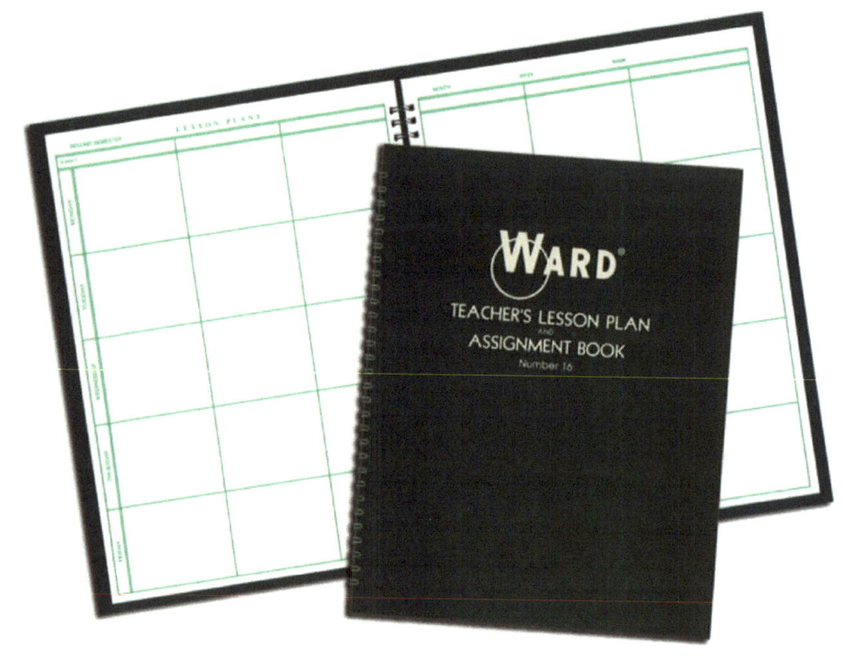

LESSON PLAN
WARD
TEACHER'S LESSON PLAN
AND
ASSIGNMENT BOOK
Number 16

COMMUNITY
OUTREACH

Chapter 7:

A LEGACY IN THE MAKING

The trials and tribulations of the past years had sculpted me into the person I had become—a passionate advocate for education and a tireless champion for underserved communities. As I reflected on the incredible journey that had brought me to this moment, I felt a profound sense of gratitude and purpose coursing through my veins. The seeds of change that had been planted during my freshman year had blossomed into a vibrant tapestry of hope and resilience, woven together by the unwavering belief that education had the power to transform lives.

Throughout my college years, I had continued to work with the summer camp, pouring my heart and soul into expanding its reach and impact. What had started as a small initiative to provide inner-city youth with a safe space to learn and grow had evolved into a transformative program that celebrated the achievements of young men who had once faced adversity. The formal gala, which had become an annual event, served as a testament to the resilience and determination of these students, showcasing their triumphs in the face of overwhelming odds.

But my work extended far beyond the confines of the summer camp. I had become a beacon of hope for those who needed it most, a guiding light in a world shrouded in darkness. Through my advocacy and outreach efforts, I sought to uplift and empower those who had been marginalized and overlooked by society, demonstrating that with perseverance and dedication, anything was possible.

As I stood on the stage during my graduation ceremony, surrounded by my peers, professors, and loved ones, I couldn't help but feel a swell of emotion wash over me. The journey of one determined educator had become a story of redemption, inspiration, and the unwavering belief that education could change lives. Each step of the way, I had been guided by a vision for a brighter future—one in which every child had access to quality education and the opportunity to fulfill their potential.

And so, with a heart full of gratitude and a vision for the future, I stepped into the next chapter of my life, ready to continue the journey of making a difference—one student, one community at a time. As I looked ahead, I knew that the road would be challenging, fraught with obstacles and setbacks. But I also knew that with perseverance and passion, I could overcome any challenge and leave a legacy that would endure for generations to come.

Chapter 8:

NAVIGATING THE PROFESSIONAL LANDSCAPE

As I transitioned from the hallowed halls of academia into the professional world of education, I was met with a stark reality that seemed to clash with the idealism of my college years. The challenges I faced were not merely academic; they were systemic, entrenched in the bureaucracy and institutional complexities of the education system.

Fresh from the cocoon of academia, I entered the classroom with a heart brimming with passion and a mind teeming with innovative ideas. However, as I navigated the professional landscape, I soon realized that my idealistic notions would be tested against the harsh realities of the education system.

One of the first challenges I encountered in my early teaching career was the delicate balance between adhering to curriculum guidelines and fostering creativity in the classroom. While curriculum guidelines provided a framework for instruction, they often left little room for flexibility or individualized learning experiences. As an advocate for student-centered education, I grappled with finding ways to infuse creativity and innovation into my lessons while still meeting the prescribed curriculum standards.

Moreover, the pervasive influence of the

standardized testing culture loomed large over the educational landscape. The relentless focus on test scores and standardized assessments seemed to overshadow the true purpose of education—to nurture critical thinking skills, foster creativity, and instill a lifelong love of learning in students. I was determined to ensure that my students received a well-rounded education that transcended mere test scores but navigating the pressures of standardized testing proved to be a formidable challenge.

Despite these obstacles, I remained steadfast in my commitment to providing my students with a holistic educational experience that encompassed not only academic learning but also social-emotional development, critical thinking skills, and real-world application of knowledge. I sought to create a classroom environment where students felt empowered to think critically, express themselves creatively, and engage in meaningful learning experiences that extended beyond the confines of standardized tests.

In order to navigate the complexities of the education system, I relied on a combination of resilience, adaptability, and a steadfast belief in the transformative power of education. I sought out professional development opportunities, collaborated with colleagues to share best practices, and advocated for policies that supported student-centered learning approaches.

As I confronted the challenges of my early teaching career, I realized that true innovation in education required not only a willingness to challenge the status quo but also a deep understanding of the systemic issues that perpetuated inequality and stifled creativity in the classroom. I remained committed to my mission of providing my students with the tools they needed to thrive in an ever-changing world, and I refused to let bureaucratic hurdles or standardized testing pressures deter me from that goal.

In the face of adversity, I drew strength from the resilience of my students, whose unwavering determination and boundless potential served as a constant source of inspiration. Together, we embarked on a journey of discovery, innovation, and transformation, determined to defy the limitations imposed by the education system and forge a new path forward toward a brighter future for all.

Chapter 9:

INNOVATIONS IN EDUCATION

Driven by a fervent passion for innovation and a relentless dedication to providing my students with the best possible learning experiences, I embarked on a journey of exploration into alternative teaching methods. As I delved into research and immersed myself in the world of educational innovation, I became increasingly convinced that traditional approaches to teaching were no longer sufficient to meet the diverse needs of today's learners. It was time to embrace new pedagogical approaches that fostered creativity, critical thinking, and collaboration.

One of the innovative teaching methods that captured my attention was project-based learning (PBL). Unlike traditional rote memorization or lecture-based instruction, PBL offered students the opportunity to engage in hands-on, real-world projects that were relevant to their interests and experiences. By framing learning within the context of authentic, meaningful projects, students were able to develop essential skills such as problem-solving, teamwork, and communication while also deepening their understanding of academic content.

Inspired by the potential of PBL to transform the learning experience, I set out to implement this approach in my own classroom. I carefully designed project-based units that challenged students to tackle complex problems, conduct research, and collaborate with their peers to develop innovative solutions. Whether it was designing sustainable cities, exploring the impact of climate change, or creating multimedia presentations on historical events, each project was carefully crafted to engage students in meaningful, inquiry-driven learning experiences.

In addition to project-based learning, I also recognized the transformative potential of technology in the classroom. In an increasingly digital world, technology had the power to revolutionize the way we teach and learn, providing access to vast resources, facilitating collaboration, and personalizing instruction to meet individual student needs. From interactive whiteboards and educational apps to online learning platforms and virtual reality simulations, technology offered endless possibilities for enhancing the educational experience.

With this in mind, I integrated technology into my teaching practice in meaningful and purposeful ways. I leveraged educational apps and digital tools to create interactive lessons, facilitate student collaboration, and provide personalized feedback. I also encouraged students to use technology as a tool for creativity and expression, empowering them to create digital media projects, design websites, and explore coding and programming languages.

Moreover, I recognized the importance of fostering a collaborative learning environment where students felt empowered to learn from one another, share ideas, and work together towards common goals. Drawing inspiration from the principles of cooperative learning and peer-to-peer collaboration, I structured my classroom as a dynamic, interactive space where students engaged in group projects, discussions, and problem-solving activities.

Through these innovative approaches to teaching and learning, I witnessed a remarkable transformation in student engagement, enthusiasm, and achievement. Students who had previously struggled in traditional classroom settings flourished in project-based environments, where they were able to apply their talents and interests in meaningful ways. Technology became not just a tool for learning but a catalyst for creativity and exploration, inspiring students to think critically, solve problems, and express themselves in new and exciting ways. And perhaps most importantly, the collaborative learning environment fostered a sense of community, belonging, and mutual support among students, laying the foundation for lifelong learning and success.

As I reflect on the journey of innovation in education, I am reminded of the profound impact that a passionate and dedicated educator can have on the lives of their students. By embracing new pedagogical approaches, leveraging technology, and fostering a collaborative learning environment, we have the power to transform education and unlock the potential of every learner. The journey of innovation is ongoing, but with perseverance, creativity, and a commitment to excellence, we can continue to push the boundaries of what is possible and create a brighter future for generations to come.

Chapter 10:

BEYOND CLASSROOM WALLS

SCHOOL

Education is a multifaceted journey that extends far beyond the confines of a traditional classroom. As an educator committed to nurturing the holistic development of my students, I embarked on a mission to break down the barriers between the school and the community, recognizing the invaluable role that external partnerships, parental involvement, and real-world experiences play in shaping the educational journey.

At the heart of this endeavor was the belief that education should not be confined to the acquisition of academic knowledge but should also encompass the development of essential life skills, character traits, and social-emotional competencies that are vital for success in the modern world. With this vision in mind, I set out to establish meaningful partnerships with local businesses, community organizations, and parents to create a comprehensive support system that would empower students to thrive both inside and outside the classroom.

One of the key components of my community engagement initiatives was the establishment of partnerships with local businesses and organizations. By forging collaborative relationships with companies and institutions in the community, I sought to provide students with real-world learning opportunities, mentorship experiences, and exposure to diverse career pathways. Through internships, job shadowing programs, and guest speaker sessions, students were able to gain valuable insights into various industries, develop professional skills, and cultivate meaningful connections that would serve them well in their future endeavors.

Additionally, I organized career workshops and informational sessions designed to equip students with the knowledge, resources, and guidance they needed to navigate the transition from school to the workforce successfully. Whether it was resume writing, interview preparation, or exploring post-secondary education options, these workshops provided students with practical tools and strategies to plan for their future and pursue their career aspirations with confidence and clarity.

Furthermore, I recognized the critical role that parental involvement plays in supporting student success and sought to actively engage parents in their children's educational journey. Through regular communication, parent-teacher conferences, and family engagement events, I fostered open lines of communication and collaboration between home and school, ensuring that parents felt empowered to play an active role in their children's education. By providing parents with resources, guidance, and opportunities for involvement, I sought to create a sense of partnership and shared responsibility for the academic and personal growth of each student.

As these community engagement initiatives took root and flourished, I witnessed a profound transformation in the educational experience of my students. By breaking down the barriers between the classroom and the community, students were able to see the relevance and real-world application of their learning, develop a deeper understanding of themselves and their aspirations, and forge meaningful connections with the world around them. Moreover, by involving parents as partners in the educational process, we were able to create a supportive ecosystem that nurtured the holistic development of each student, fostering a sense of belonging, purpose, and resilience that would serve them well beyond their time in school.

As I reflect on the impact of these initiatives, I am reminded of the power of community partnerships, parental involvement, and real-world experiences in enriching the educational journey and empowering students to reach their full potential. By expanding the boundaries of education beyond the classroom walls and embracing the collective strength of the community, we can create a more inclusive, equitable, and empowering educational experience for all students, laying the foundation for a brighter future for generations to come.

Chapter 11:

ADVOCATING FOR SYSTEMIC CHANGE

Youth participation
Advocacy
Policy

As I progressed in my career as an educator, I came to realize that while making a difference at the individual level was profoundly gratifying, it was imperative to address the systemic issues that perpetuated inequality and hindered the educational opportunities of marginalized communities. Inspired by a deep sense of social responsibility and a commitment to equity, I embarked on a journey of advocacy, joining forces with like-minded educators to push for systemic changes that would create a more just and inclusive educational landscape.

Advocacy became a significant aspect of my career, as I recognized that effecting meaningful change required more than just passion and dedication—it necessitated strategic action and collective mobilization. I sought to leverage my position and expertise to advocate for policy changes, equitable resource allocation, and a curriculum that embraced diversity and inclusion, thereby dismantling the systemic barriers that impeded the academic success and well-being of underserved students.

One of the key areas of advocacy was policy reform. Recognizing the pivotal role that education policy plays in shaping the educational experiences of students, I collaborated with policymakers, advocacy groups, and community stakeholders to advocate for policies that promoted equity, fostered inclusivity, and prioritized the needs of historically marginalized populations. Whether it was advocating for increased funding for low-income schools, advocating for culturally responsive teaching practices, or advocating for policies that addressed the root causes of educational inequity, I worked tirelessly to ensure that the voices of those most affected by systemic injustice were heard and amplified in the policymaking process.

Equally important was the fight for equitable resource allocation. I recognized that disparities in funding, resources, and support services perpetuated educational inequities and entrenched systemic barriers to success. Thus, I became a vocal advocate for fair and equitable resource allocation, urging policymakers and educational leaders to prioritize the needs of underserved schools and communities. Whether it was advocating for increased funding for essential resources such as textbooks, technology, and classroom supplies or fighting for access to high-quality facilities, extracurricular programs, and support services, I sought to level the playing field and ensure that all students had the resources and support they needed to thrive academically and personally.

Furthermore, I championed a curriculum that

embraced diversity, equity, and inclusion. I recognized that traditional curricula often marginalized the histories, cultures, and experiences of marginalized communities, perpetuating harmful stereotypes and erasing the contributions of diverse voices. Thus, I advocated for the integration of culturally relevant content, diverse perspectives, and inclusive pedagogies into the curriculum, ensuring that students saw themselves reflected in the materials they studied and that their identities and experiences were affirmed and celebrated in the classroom. By advocating for a curriculum that honored the richness and diversity of human experience, I sought to empower students to become critical thinkers, compassionate global citizens, and agents of change in their communities and beyond.

As I engaged in advocacy efforts, I encountered numerous challenges and obstacles along the way. Bureaucratic inertia, political resistance, and entrenched interests often stood in the way of progress, requiring persistence, resilience, and strategic collaboration to overcome. Yet, I remained undeterred, drawing strength from the knowledge that the work we were doing was not just about advocating for change but about transforming lives and building a more just and equitable society for future generations.

Despite the challenges, our advocacy efforts began to yield tangible results. Policy reforms were enacted, funding allocations were increased, and curriculum changes were implemented, leading to greater equity, inclusivity, and opportunity for all students. While there is still much work to be done, I am proud of the progress we have made and inspired by the collective power of educators, activists, and advocates to effect positive change in the world.

As I continue on my journey of advocacy, I am reminded of the words of Margaret Mead: "Never doubt that a small group of thoughtful, committed citizens can change the world; indeed, it's the only thing that ever has." With this mantra guiding my work, I remain committed to advocating for systemic change, dismantling systemic barriers, and creating a more just and equitable educational system that affirms the inherent worth and dignity of every student, regardless of their background, identity, or circumstances.

Chapter 12:

THE IMPACT UNFOLDS

Amidst the complexities of navigating systemic challenges and the tireless efforts in advocating for change, the true measure of our work as educators lay in the transformative impact it had on the lives of students. As I continued to navigate the educational landscape, the unfolding stories of triumph, resilience, and empowerment among my students served as poignant reminders of the profound significance of our collective endeavors.

Success stories began to emerge, each one a testament to the resilience and tenacity of the human spirit. I witnessed students who, despite facing daunting obstacles and systemic barriers, refused to succumb to the limitations imposed upon them. Instead, they defied expectations, shattered stereotypes, and charted their own paths towards success. From overcoming economic hardship to navigating familial challenges, these students demonstrated unwavering determination and perseverance in the pursuit of their dreams.

One such story was that of Maria, a first-generation immigrant student who arrived in the United States with limited English proficiency and faced numerous barriers to academic success. Despite the odds stacked against her, Maria refused to be defined by her circumstances. With the support of dedicated educators and mentors, she immersed herself in her studies, tirelessly honing her language skills and academic abilities. Through sheer grit and determination, Maria not only mastered English but excelled academically, earning a scholarship to attend college—a feat once deemed unimaginable.

Similarly, there was Jamal, a young man from an underserved neighborhood plagued by poverty and violence. Growing up, Jamal confronted myriad challenges, including the lack of access to quality education and the pervasive influence of negative peer pressures. However, Jamal refused to be a product of his environment. With the guidance of caring educators and community mentors, he discovered his passion for entrepreneurship and began to envision a future beyond the confines of his circumstances. Through perseverance and hard work, Jamal launched his own business, providing employment opportunities for members of his community and serving as a beacon of hope for others trapped in cycles of poverty and despair.

These success stories, and countless others like them, underscored the transformative power of education and the profound impact that dedicated educators can have on the lives of their students. They served as living embodiments of the resilience, determination, and potential that resides within every individual, regardless of their background or circumstances.

As I bore witness to these stories of triumph and transformation, my determination to persevere in the face of systemic resistance was reignited. The challenges we faced in advocating for systemic change paled in comparison to the indomitable spirit of our students, who refused to be defined by the limitations imposed upon them. Their stories served as powerful reminders of the imperative to continue our efforts to dismantle systemic barriers, expand access to quality education, and create opportunities for all students to thrive.

Moreover, the impact of our collective efforts extended far beyond the individual students we served—it reverberated throughout entire communities, catalyzing positive change and fostering a culture of hope and possibility. As students graduated, pursued higher education, and embarked on successful careers, they became agents of change in their own right, paying it forward and inspiring future generations to dream big and reach for the stars.

In the end, the true measure of our success as educators lay not in test scores or academic accolades but in the lives we touched and the futures we helped to shape. As we continued to bear witness to the unfolding impact of our work, I was reminded of the words of Nelson Mandela, who once said, "Education is the most powerful weapon which you can use to change the world." Indeed, the impact of education is profound, far-reaching, and enduring—a beacon of hope in a world fraught with challenges and uncertainties. And as we journeyed forward, guided by a shared commitment to equity, justice, and empowerment, the impact of our collective efforts continued to unfold, illuminating the path towards a brighter, more inclusive future for all.

Chapter 13:

THE NEXT GENERATION OF EDUCATORS

As I reflected on my own journey in education, I realized that passing on the torch to the next generation of educators was not only a natural progression but also a profound responsibility. Mentoring aspiring teachers and future leaders in education became a cornerstone of my mission—a way to ensure that the values of resilience, innovation, and a commitment to making a lasting impact on education were carried forward into the future.

Mentorship, I believed, was more than just imparting knowledge or sharing experiences; it was about nurturing potential, fostering growth, and inspiring a new generation of change-makers. As I embarked on this journey of mentorship, I was filled with a sense of purpose and excitement, knowing that I had the opportunity to shape the trajectory of aspiring educators and empower them to effect positive change in their communities.

One of the first mentees I had the privilege of working with was Michael, a bright and passionate young man with a deep-seated desire to make a difference in the field of education. Like me, Michael had experienced firsthand the transformative power of education in his own life, and he was determined to pay it forward by becoming a teacher. However, he was unsure of how to navigate the complexities of the education system and overcome the challenges that lay ahead.

Through our mentorship relationship, I provided Michael with guidance, support, and encouragement as he navigated his journey in education. We discussed strategies for classroom management, innovative teaching techniques, and ways to foster a culture of inclusivity and equity in his future classroom. I shared my own experiences, both triumphs and challenges, and offered insights gained from years of working in the field.

Over time, I watched with pride as Michael blossomed into a confident and capable educator, armed with the knowledge, skills, and passion needed to make a meaningful impact in the lives of his students. He embraced new ideas, experimented with innovative teaching methods, and remained steadfast in his commitment to creating a supportive and empowering learning environment for all students.

But Michael was just one of many mentees I had the privilege of working with over the years. Each one brought their own unique perspectives, experiences, and aspirations to the table, enriching the mentorship experience and reminding me of the boundless potential that exists within the next generation of educators.

Together, we explored new frontiers in education, pushing the boundaries of traditional teaching methods and embracing innovation as a catalyst for positive change. We discussed the role of technology in the classroom, the importance of culturally responsive teaching practices, and the need for greater diversity and representation in the education workforce. Through collaborative brainstorming sessions and hands-on workshops, we developed creative solutions to address the myriad challenges facing educators today.

But perhaps the most rewarding aspect of mentorship was witnessing the ripple effect of positive influence as my mentees went on to inspire others in turn. Like a pebble dropped into a pond, each mentee carried forward the values and lessons they had learned, touching the lives of countless students, colleagues, and community members along the way.

As I looked towards the future, I felt a sense of hope and optimism knowing that the next generation of educators was in good hands. Together, we had planted the seeds of change, nurturing them with care and dedication, and watching them grow into a thriving ecosystem of innovation, empowerment, and excellence in education.

But our work was far from done. As mentors and mentees alike, we recognized the importance of continuous learning and growth, of remaining open to new ideas and perspectives, and of always striving to be the best educators we could be. For it was only through collaboration, resilience, and a shared commitment to excellence that we could truly make a lasting impact on the future of education and, by extension, the world.

In the end, mentorship was not just about passing on knowledge or skills—it was about passing on a legacy of hope, inspiration, and possibility. It was about empowering the next generation to believe in themselves, to dream big, and to never lose sight of the incredible potential that lies within each and every one of us. And as I continued on my own journey, I knew that the greatest legacy I could leave behind was not in the accolades or achievements, but in the lives I touched and the hearts I inspired along the way.

BLACK
EDUCATORS
MATTER

Chapter 14:

REFLECTIONS AND LEGACY

As I sit down to reflect on the expansive journey that has brought me from a struggling teenager to an educator advocating for systemic change, I am filled with a profound sense of gratitude and humility. The path I have traveled has been filled with highs and lows, victories and defeats, but through it all, one thing has remained constant: my unwavering belief in the transformative power of education.

Education, I have come to realize, is not just about imparting knowledge or mastering skills; it is about empowering individuals to realize their full potential, to overcome obstacles, and to create positive change in their own lives and the lives of others. It is a tool for liberation, a pathway to opportunity, and a cornerstone of a just and equitable society.

As I reflect on my own journey, I am reminded of the countless individuals who have helped shape my path and inspire my passion for education. From teachers who believed in me when I doubted myself to mentors who guided me with wisdom and compassion, each person has played a role in shaping the educator I am today.

But perhaps the most significant influence on my journey has been the students themselves—the young minds and hearts that I have had the privilege of teaching, mentoring, and learning from. Their resilience, creativity, and boundless potential have fueled my determination to advocate for change and challenge the status quo.

In crafting this narrative, my intention is not just to recount a personal journey but to inspire others to persist in their pursuits of positive change. Education, I believe, is the great equalizer—the key to unlocking doors of opportunity and building a brighter future for all. But realizing this vision requires courage, determination, and a willingness to confront the systemic barriers that stand in the way of progress.

Throughout my career, I have encountered myriad challenges and obstacles—limited resources, bureaucratic hurdles, and entrenched inequities—that threaten to undermine the promise of education. Yet, in the face of adversity, I have remained steadfast in my commitment to effecting change, drawing strength from the resilience of my students and the power of collective action.

Education, I have come to realize, is not a solitary endeavor but a collaborative effort that requires the collective engagement of educators, students, families, and communities. It is about building bridges, forging partnerships, and creating a shared vision for a more just and equitable society.

As I look back on the legacy I am building, I am reminded of the words of Nelson Mandela: "Education is the most powerful weapon which you can use to change the world." It is a sentiment that resonates deeply with me, for I believe that education has the power to transform lives, uplift communities, and catalyze social change.

But the work is far from over. As I continue on my journey, I am reminded of the countless individuals who are still denied access to quality education, the systemic injustices that persist in our schools and communities, and the urgent need for collective action to address these challenges.

As educators, advocates, and changemakers, we have a responsibility to ensure that every child has the opportunity to receive a quality education, regardless of their race, ethnicity, socioeconomic status, or zip code. We must confront the disparities that exist in our education system, dismantle the structures of oppression that perpetuate inequality, and create a more just and equitable future for all.

In the end, the legacy I hope to leave behind is not measured in accolades or achievements but in the lives I have touched, the hearts I have inspired, and the positive change I have helped to effect in the world. And as I continue on this journey, I am filled with hope and optimism knowing that the transformative power of education will continue to shine bright, lighting the way for future generations to come

Conclusion:

THE EVER-EVOLVING JOURNEY

As I reflect on the pages of this chronicle, tracing the trajectory of my journey from a struggling teenager to an advocate for systemic change in education, I am reminded that the story is far from over. Indeed, the landscape of education is ever-evolving, and the challenges we face are as complex as they are daunting. Yet, it is within these challenges that the seeds of innovation, resilience, and lasting change are sown.

Throughout this narrative, I have shared the triumphs and tribulations, the moments of inspiration and the periods of doubt that have defined my path as an educator. From the formative experiences of my youth to the pivotal moments of my career, each chapter has contributed to the tapestry of my journey, shaping the educator I am today.

But this story is not just mine alone. It is a testament to the enduring spirit of countless individuals—teachers, mentors, colleagues, and students—who have played a role in shaping my journey and inspiring my passion for education. It is a tribute to the collective power of those who believe in the profound impact of education on shaping a better future.

As I conclude this narrative, I am filled with a sense of gratitude for the opportunities I have been afforded, the lessons I have learned, and the relationships I have forged along the way. But I am also acutely aware of the work that remains to be done.

The journey of education is a never-ending one, marked by progress and setbacks, breakthroughs and challenges. It is a journey that requires courage, perseverance, and an unwavering commitment to the principles of equity, justice, and inclusion.

May this chronicle serve as a beacon of hope for those who dare to dream and strive to make a difference in the world of education. May it inspire future generations of educators, advocates, and changemakers to carry forward the torch of progress, to confront the injustices that persist, and to envision a future where every child has the opportunity to thrive.

The journey continues, and the story unfolds with each new chapter, written by those who dare to dream and strive to make a difference. As we embark on the next phase of this ever-evolving journey, let us do so with humility, determination, and a steadfast belief in the transformative power of education to shape a better world for all.

EVERY NEXT LEVEL OF
YOUR LIFE WILL DEMAND
A DIFFERENT YOU

UNKNOWN

Babita Spinelli